countries that have surprised me the most in my travels. It is incredible all that such a small country has to offer:

1. The biodiversity of the Amazon.

2. The roads, cities and mountain landscapes in the Andes region.

3. The Pacific coast region.

4. And the crown jewel of Ecuador: the Galapagos Islands.

My name is Alberto Barambio Canet, a passionate traveler who creates travel content under the name '1 Hour Travel Guides'. In 2021, I set a goal to share my travel experiences and inspire more people to live beyond their 9-5pm office job.

For 75 days I was living in Quito and traveling around Ecuador. With this guide you will be able to plan your trip in a faster and easier way. In just one document or book, I offer you the best routes and all the basics you need to

This book is dedicated to my Ecuadorian friends Chiara Stornaiolo, Bianca Yépez and Lorena Darquea whom I met in Bogotá, Colombia. For encouraging me to travel through Ecuador and to love the country before I even set foot in it.

1 HOUR TRAVEL GUIDES

✉ ABARAMBIO1@GMAIL.COM

f 1HOURTRAVELGUIDES

◎ @1HOURTRAVELGUIDES

➤ LINKTR.EE/1HOURTRAVELGUIDES

CUENCA

Index

TUNGURAHUA VOLCANO
(BAÑOS)

Introduction

All recommendations and advice in this book come from my own research and experiences traveling in Ecuador.

Although I have written the book with the utmost care, I cannot guarantee that the content is completely free of minor errors. Therefore, "A viajar, que son dos días" is free from erroneous or outdated information.

If you liked the book, it would be helpful if you could leave a review on Amazon. Comments are an important way for other readers to discover the book. Your opinion and experience can be valuable in helping others decide if the book is right for them. Thanks for your support!

Before your trip

ECUADOR TRAVEL INSPIRATION | INFO ABOUT
ECUADOR | CULTURAL INSPIRATION | WEATHER
AND BEST TIME TO GO | TRAVEL PREPARATIONS

Ecuador
Travel inspiration

Books

GALÁPAGOS
Kurt Vonnegut

HUASIPUNGO
Jorge Icaza

Movies

RATAS, RATONES Y RATEROS
Sebastián Cordero

EL ÚLTIMO HIELERO
Sandy Patch

Music

TRAVEL ECUADOR
Spotify QR code

LAS GRIETAS

Mindo ★

★ Quito

★ Cotopaxi

Cuyabeno
Amazon

Montañita
★

Baños ★

★ Guayaquil

★ Cuenca

Ecuador

Galapagos
Islands
★

Did you know...?

Ecuador is the world's largest exporter of bananas, with almost 25% of world production.

Ecuador is one of the 13 countries in the world that crosses the equator hence its name.

The only way to live in Galapagos is to be born on the island or to marry a native of the islands.

The dollar was established in the year 2000, replacing the sucre to combat inflation and stabilize the economy.

The hours of sunshine in Ecuador are year-round from 6 am to 6 pm.

Did you know...?

The capital of Ecuador is Quito, although the most populated city is Guayaquil. Ecuador has a population of 17.5 million.

Its language is Spanish. The currency is the U.S. dollar.

The main religion is Christianity (Catholic religion). But Ecuador is a secular state.

Ecuador operates with plug A and B. The voltage is 120V and 60 Hz.

Quito is the second highest capital city in the world at 2,850 meters (9,350 feet) above sea level.

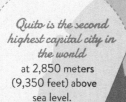

9,350 ft

Weather
and best time to go

CLIMATE IN ECUADOR

The **climate** in Ecuador is **influenced** by its **proximity** to the **equator** and its **varied topography**: mountains, coast, islands and jungle.

These are the **climates according** to their **ecosystem**:

HIGHLANDS (ANDES REGION)

- The climate is **cool** due to the **altitude**.
- **Temperatures** between **7-22 °C** (45-72 °F).

AMAZON

- **Warm** and **humid** all year round.
- **Temperatures** between 22-30 °C (72-86 °F)
- **Rainy season** is from **March to July**.

COAST

- **Warm** and **humid** climate all year round.
- **Temperatures** between 25-32 °C (77-90 °F).
- **Rainy season** from December to May.

GALAPAGOS

- **Warm** temperatures all year round (average 25°C).

- **Warm season**: extends from December to May. Rainier climate. Water temperature is warmer and perfect for diving.

- **Cool season**: June to November. Drier and cooler weather. Cooler water temperature, making it perfect for bird and animal watching.

Destinations	JAN	FEB	MAR	APR	MAY	JUN	JUL	AUG	SEP	OCT	NOV	DEC
Quito												
Mindo												
Cotopaxi												
Cuenca												
Baños												
Galapagos												
Montañita												
Guayaquil												
Amazon												

Best Weather   Ok   Worst

Highlands   Galapagos   Coast   Amazon

14

Travel

preparations

WITHOUT VISA

If you are **European** or a citizen of the **American continent** (except Venezuela and Cuba):

- You do **not** need a **visa**.
- You do **not** have to **pay** anything at the entrance to Ecuador.
- You simply receive a stamp in your passport.

VISA

Many countries in **Asia** and **Africa** do **require** a **visa**. In the link below you can find all the countries on the list, requirements, costs and procedures:

https://visaguide.world/south-america/ecuador-visa/

HOW CAN YOU ENTER ECUADOR WITHOUT A VISA

- With a **passport valid** for **more** than **6 months**.
- You must have a **ticket** to **leave** the **country**.
- **Travel insurance** valid during your stay.

FREQUENTLY ASKED QUESTIONS

- **¿How many days** can I stay in Ecuador as a **tourist?** 90 days.
- **Can I extend my stay** in Ecuador? Yes, you can request an extension of 90 days (180 days per year).

CUENCA

SPECIAL VISA

Keep in mind that you need a **special visa** to travel to the **Galapagos** Islands. This can only be purchased at the **Quito** and **Guayaquil airports**. It costs **$20** and can be found at the check-in area of the airports.

Travel *preparations*

MUST-HAVE APPLICATIONS ON YOUR PHONE

- **Uber / Didi / Cabify**

These apps are essential to **order** a **cab** in Ecuador. I recommend you **compare prices** between the 3 since their rates often change. It is **much safer** to order a cab through these apps, than to get in a cab on the street.

- **Google Maps / Maps.me**

These 2 **map applications** are very useful to move about easily in your destinations. **Download** the maps of Ecuador to use it offline.

- **XE currency**

To know the **conversion from US dollar** to your own currency.

- **Uber Eats**

This is the best app in Ecuador to order **food delivery**. Among the destinations I recommend, it works in Cuenca, Quito and Guayaquil.

- **Splitwise**

Great app if you travel in company. It is useful to **keep track** of the trip **costs** and **divide expenses**.

- **Shark count**

The app is perfect for **divers**. It reports how many **sightings** of **sharks, whales** and other marine species and their location in Galapagos.

WIFI

The Wi-Fi's connection in Ecuador can vary depending on the destination of your trip:

- The connection is **good** in **larger cities** such as Quito, Guayaquil and Cuenca.

- In destinations like **Mindo, Montañita** or **Baños**, it **depends** on the **hotel** where you stay.

- In **Galapagos**, the connection is **poor**. There are often interruptions and video calls are often complicated.

- In **highland** destinations such as **Cotopaxi**, some accommodations **may not have Wi-Fi**.

- In the **Amazon** region, it is **likely** that you will **not** have any **connection** at all in the accommodations.

TARJETA SIM

Upon arrival at the airport, you can buy the chip for your phone.

The most popular **phone companies** in Ecuador are:

- Claro
- Movistar
- CNT
- Tuenti

The company with the **best signal** is **Claro**. Especially in the Galapagos Islands.

Keep in mind that **coverage** in certain **mountainous areas** and the **Amazon** is low or **non-existent**.

Preparations *for your trip*

TRAVEL INSURANCE

Although it is unlikely that you will be asked to show it, travel **insurance** is a **mandatory** requirement to enter Ecuador.

The insurance I use on my trips is the '**Safetywing**' insurance:

- It **covers** accidents **up** to **$250,000**.
- It only **costs $16/10 days**.
- It has **24-hour customer service**.
- The times I have had to make claims, I have had no problems covering medical expenses.

VACCINATIONS

Although there are **no mandatory vaccinations** to enter Ecuador, the World Health Organization **recommends** the following:

- Hepatitis A
- Hepatitis B
- Varicella
- Influenza
- Measles
- Tdap (Tetanus, diphtheria and pertussis)
- MMR (Meningitis, mumps and rubella)
- Typhoid fever
- Yellow fever

*Be very careful with mosquito bites in the Amazon (there is a **risk** of **malaria** and **dengue**).

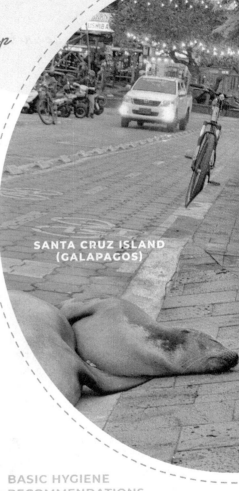

SANTA CRUZ ISLAND (GALAPAGOS)

BASIC HYGIENE RECOMMENDATIONS

- In **Quito** and **Guayaquil**, you **can drink tap water** (although it is not recommended if you are not used to it). In all **other destinations**, tap water is **not good** for your health.

- Wash your hands frequently

- Beware of uncooked food or street stalls that look unhygienic.

Preparations *for your trip*

TIPS FOR YOUR LUGGAGE

Keep in mind these **tips** for **packing** your suitcase:

1) **Check the weather**: you may need warm clothes to go to highland destinations. Lighter clothes and swimsuit if you go to Galapagos and coast and clothes that are breathable and lightweight if you go to the Amazon.

2) **Adequate clothing**: depending on the places you visit; it is important that you wear adequate clothing. Keep in mind if you will be hiking, doing outdoor activities or plan to visit coastal areas.

3) **Comfortable shoes**: for walking in the cities or even hiking if that is your plan.

4) **Sunscreen and repellent**: it is important to leave home with sunscreen. Because it is located close to the equator, the sun burns a lot in this country. Also don't forget to use mosquito repellent to protect yourself from diseases on the coast and Amazon.

5) **Adapter**: don't forget to bring an adapter to be able to use your electronic devices in Ecuador.

*DON'T FORGET

- That your **passport** should be **valid** for **at least 6 months**.
- Organize and keep your travel documents in an easily accessible place.
- Download and **test** the **phone apps** before traveling.
- Always **carry this book** in your **suitcase**.

List

DOCUMENTS

- Passport
- Wallet
- Credit/debit card
- Travel insurance
- Copy of important documents

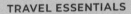

TRAVEL ESSENTIALS

- Backpack or suitcase
- Daytrip backpack
- Money belt
- Microfiber towel
- Flip flops
- Walking shoes
- Hiking shoes
- Universal adapter
- Padlock

ELECTRONIC PRODUCTS

- Camera and memory cards
- Power bank
- Phone
- Chargers

CLOTHING

- Hat
- Sweatshirt
- 1 jacket (winter)
- Swimming suit
- 1 long-sleeved T-shirt
- Long pants
- Shorts and t-shirts
- Underwear
- 1 dress/shirt
- Raincoat
- Sunglasses
- Belt

PERSONAL CARE PRODUCTS

- Sunscreen
- Mosquito repellent
- Antibacterial gel
- Deodorant
- Toothbrush and toothpaste
- Razor
- Femenine hygiene products
- Hair brush
- Paracetamol
- Diarrhea tablets

PLAZA SAN FRANCISCO
(QUITO)

1 week
itinerary

Quito

Baños

Cuenca

**Map:
1 week
itinerary**

Galapagos
Islands

1 week itinerary
(3 destinations)

Before talking about the route, you should know the easiest and most **common way** to **get** to **Ecuador**:

- Mariscal Sucre International **Airport (Quito).**
- José Joaquín Olmedo **Airport (Guayaquil).**

These are the 2 points where travelers usually start their trip.

Ecuador has 4 **main zones**:

1. HIGHLANDS
Quito, Mindo, Cotopaxi, Cuenca and Baños.

- - - - - - - - - - - - - - - -

2. GALAPAGOS ISLANDS

3. COSTA PACÍFICO
Guayaquil and Montañita.

4. AMAZON

Ecuadorians often refer to these areas as the "**four worlds** of **Ecuador**". This is because they have **4** totally different **ecosystems**.

DAY 1 QUITO

Quito is the **capital** of Ecuador. It is located in the **Andes** region, in the **north** of the country.

There you can enjoy its impressive **colonial architecture**, its rich history and of course, its breathtaking **panoramic view** from the top of the Pichincha volcano. You can also visit its beautiful gardens, parks and **squares**, as well as its vibrant local **markets** and stores.

Be prepared for the **altitude**, however, as Quito is more than **2,800 m**. (9,200 ft) above sea level.

IGLESIA DE LA COMPAÑIA

1 week itinerary
(3 destinations)

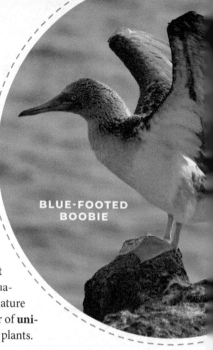

BLUE-FOOTED BOOBIE

DAY 3-5 GALAPAGOS

Take a **flight** from Quito to the Galapagos Islands, the jewel of Ecuador.

Visitors travel by plane from the capital of Ecuador, **Quito**, **or** from the city of **Guayaquil**.

The Galapagos Islands are an **archipelago** located in the Pacific Ocean, about **1,300 km** (800 miles) off the coast of Ecuador. They are a popular destination for nature lovers, as they are home to a large number of **unique** and endemic species of **animals** and plants.

Transportation from
QUITO TO GALAPAGOS

 PLANE | 3.5 HOURS, $190-600

OPTIONS
- Layover in Guayaquil
- Airport: Baltra island
- Airport: San Cristobal island

DAY 6 CUENCA/BAÑOS

If you **only** have **a week** in your visit, I recommend that you **choose between** the cities of **Cuenca and Baños**.

Cuenca is a colonial city full of **history** and architectural beauty.

Baños, on the other hand, is recommended for **nature** lovers: hiking, waterfalls and adventure activities.

CUENCA'S CATHEDRAL

Transportation from
GALAPAGOS

 PLANE | 1 H 50 MIN
Flight to Guayaquil

 BUS
To Cuenca (4 hours)
To Baños (6 hours)

1 week itinerary
(3 destinations)

DAY 7 QUITO

On your **last day**, you can take the opportunity to continue exploring the colonial architecture, go to bazaars to buy **souvenirs** of your trip or continue experiencing the delicious **Ecuadorian food**. This way you can say goodbye to Ecuador in the best possible way.

Transportation to
QUITO

✈ **AIRPLANE**
Cuenca: 50 MIN, $40

🚌 **BUS**
- *Baños:* 3 H. 15 MIN, $6
- *Cuenca:* 8 HOURS, $20

BASÍLICA DEL
VOTO NACIONAL

Mindo ★

★ Quito

Cuyabeno
Amazonas ★

★ Cotopaxi

Montañita

Baños ★

★ Guayaquil

★ Cuenca

Map:
3 weeks
itinerary

Galapagos
Islands
★

3 weeks itinerary
(9 destinations)

DAY 1-2 QUITO

Quito is the **capital** of Ecuador. It is located in the **Andes region (north)**.

There you can enjoy its impressive **colonial architecture**, its rich history and of course, its breathtaking **panoramic view** from the top of the Pichincha volcano. You can also visit its beautiful gardens, parks and plazas, as well as its vibrant local **markets** and stores.

Be prepared for the **altitude**, however, as Quito is more than **2,800 meters** (9,200 ft) above sea level.

DAY 3-7 GALAPAGOS

Take a **flight** from Quito to the Galapagos Islands, the jewel of Ecuador.

The Galapagos Islands are an **archipelago** located in the Pacific Ocean, about **1,300 km** (800 miles) off the coast. They are a popular destination for **nature lovers**, as they are home to a large number of **endemic species**.

Transportation from
QUITO TO GALÁPAGOS

 PLANE | 3.5 HOURS, $190-600

OPTIONS
-Layover in Guayaquil
-Airport: Baltra island
-Airport: San Cristobal airport

DAY 9-10 GUAYAQUIL

Time to enjoy another ecosystem in Ecuador: the **coastal region**.

In Guayaquil you can visit the famous **Iguanas Park**, stroll along the **Malecón** or enjoy a different view of the city from its **cable car**.

Transportation
 GALAPAGOS TO GUAYAQUIL

 PLANE | 1H 50 MIN

GUAYAQUIL

3 weeks itinerary
(9 destinations)

DAY 9-10 MONTAÑITA

In just 3 hours you can get from Guayaquil to the **second destination** of your trip along the **coast**.

There you can enjoy a **perfect climate all year** round. Perfect destination for **surfing** and going out at night to its many **nightclubs**.

Transportation from
GUAYAQUIL TO MONTAÑITA

 BUS | 3H, $18
Recommended option

 TAXI | 2H 15 MIN, $100

CAJAS NATIONAL PARK (CUENCA)

DAY 11-12 CUENCA

Time to return to the **highlands** and the **third largest city** in Ecuador.

A visit to Cuenca is an opportunity to experience the rich **history** and culture of this country. The city is known for its impressive **colonial buildings** and architecture.

In addition, I recommend a day trip to **Cajas National Park**.

Transportation from
MONTAÑITA TO CUENCA

 BUS | 7 H 30 MIN, $40

The simplest route:
- Montañita-Guayaquil
- Guayaquil-Cuenca

3 weeks itinerary
(9 destinations)

DAY 13-14 BAÑOS

Baños is a popular tourist destination known for its **mountain scenery** and **adventure** activities.

It is a perfect place for those looking for a **combination** of **relaxation** and **adventure**: there you can enjoy a variety of activities, from relaxing in hot springs, to cycling along a waterfall trail.

Transportation from
CUENCA TO BAÑOS

 BUS | 4H 40 MIN, $15
Recommended option

DAY 15-16 COTOPAXI

Cotopaxi National Park is a national park in the highlands of the Andes. It is also a **volcano** with high activity.

The park offers different trails with spectacular **scenery**. It is also perfect for climbing enthusiasts and **adventure** lovers.

Transportation from
BAÑOS TO COTOPAXI

 BUS | 4 H, $5

* The best option is to get to the town of Machachi. From there you can take local bus or cab.

3 weeks itinerary
(9 destinations)

DAY 17-19 AMAZON

There are **4 zones** to have your **Amazon** experience:

- Tena
- Puyo
- Yasani
- Cuyabeno

Tena and **Puyo** are found shortly after you enter the jungle. So, it will be a **cheaper** experience, but **less authentic**. There are fewer options to see animals.

Yasuní and **Cuyabeno** are much further into the Amazon. There are **fewer tourists**, and **more animals** can be seen.

Transportation from
QUITO TO THE AMAZON

 BUS/AIRPLANE

The most common way to go is by bus. Although you can get to Yasuní flying to "Coca".

DAY 20 MINDO

This is a destination for **nature** lovers. It is known for its **cloud forest** and its diversity of **birds**. It is popular for **hiking**, tubing, exploring biking trails and tasting **coffee** and chocolate.

Transportation from
QUITO TO MINDO

 BUS | 3.5 H, $4
Recommended option

 TAXI: 1.5 H, $55

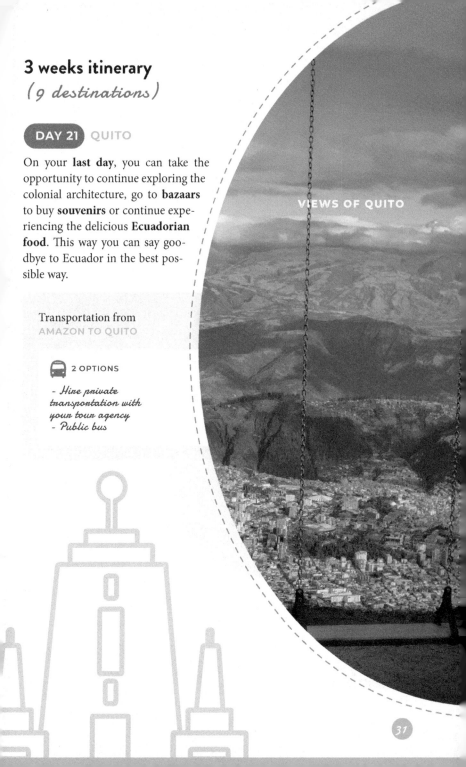

3 weeks itinerary
(9 destinations)

DAY 21 QUITO

On your **last day**, you can take the opportunity to continue exploring the colonial architecture, go to **bazaars** to buy **souvenirs** or continue experiencing the delicious **Ecuadorian food**. This way you can say goodbye to Ecuador in the best possible way.

Transportation from
AMAZON TO QUITO

2 OPTIONS

- *Hire private transportation with your tour agency*
- *Public bus*

VIEWS OF QUITO

Best places to visit

Quito

⛅ BEST TIME TO GO
JUNE-OCTOBER

Quito is the **capital** of Ecuador and the **first stop** on your **trip** to Ecuador. It is located in the Ecuadorian highlands, **surrounded** by **mountains** and with a breathtaking view of the Andes Mountains.

The city is known for its important center with colonial architecture and cobblestone streets. It is also a popular destination for food lovers.

It is also a **key connecting point** in your trip: from there you can get directly to any destination in the guide except Montañita.

AQUÍ
LA CULTURA
SE VIVE

Ecuador en la mitad del mundo

Latitud 00°00'00

Calculada con G.P.S.

MUSEO DE SITIO INTIÑAN

Camino del sol

Latitud: 00°00'00"

INTIÑÁN MUSEUM

What to do *Quito*

1. MIDDLE OF THE WORLD

Only **40 minutes from Quito**, north of the city. You can find **2 museums**:

- Mitad del Mundo Museum.
- Intiñan Museum.

You can visit the **equator line** that separates the northern hemisphere from the southern hemisphere. You can also attend **scientific experiments**.

2. LA MARISCAL MARKET

Perfect market in Quito to **buy handicrafts** and **souvenirs**. There is a great variety of handicraft products typical of Ecuador. There you can buy various items from traditional clothing of Ecuador to jewelry or decoration for your home.

3. HISTORICAL CENTER

One of the best preserved in Latin America. Declared a World Heritage Site, it has beautiful **colonial churches**, **squares** and cobblestone alleys.

Visit the top of the **Basilica** del Voto Nacional, the **Plaza Grande**, **Plaza** de **San Francisco** and the **Panecillo**.

RUCU PICHINCHA

4. MUSEUMS

I recommend the **Guayasamin Museum** (Oswaldo Guayas' museum) and Museum of **Pre-Columbian Art** (with more than 5,000 pieces of past societies in Ecuador).

5. QUITO CABLE CAR

It takes you to the highest point of the city (**4,000 meters/13,100 ft**). From there you have spectacular **views** of the **city** and the Andes Mountain range.

From there you can **climb** to the **summit** of **Pichincha** (4,784 meters/15,700 ft). The ascent takes about 3 hours.

-**Price**: $9.

-**Hours**: Monday-Friday (9:00-19:00) and Saturday-Sunday (8:00-19:00).

What to do *Quito*

🍽️ *Restaurants*

1. **CAFÉ MOSAICO** $

2. **DE LA LLAMA** $-$$

3. **CASA WARMI** $$

4. **MERCADO CENTRAL** $

HISTORICAL CENTER

🛏️ *Hotels*

COMMUNITY HOSTEL $

Located in the center of Quito. Close to tourist attractions. It has a large community of travelers.

SELINA QUITO $$

Hostel with an excellent location and perfect if you are traveling and need to work.

MIDDLE OF THE WORLD MUSEUM

💬 *Prices*

$ = UP TO $15
$$ = $15-50
$$$ = FROM $50

Vegan Options

Galapagos

☀ BEST TIME TO GO
JUNE-SEPTEMBER

These **islands**, located in the Pacific Ocean west of Ecuador, are known for their **biodiversity** and for being home to many **endemic species**, including marine iguanas, giant tortoises, and birds such as Darwin's finch.

They also offer **breathtaking scenery**, such as **white sand beaches** and **active volcanoes**. Although you can travel on your own to the Galapagos, most travelers explore the islands by cruise ship or with tours.

Santa Cruz *Island*

1. CHARLES DARWIN CENTER

Here you can see **giant tortoises bred** at the center and visit the **embalmed body** of the last tortoise of his species: **Lonesome George**.

2. TORTUGA BAY

Beautiful **white sand beach**. It can be reached by walking and is one of the best **free activities**. On this beach you can find **sea lions, iguanas, blue-footed boobies**, **turtles** and **sharks** while snorkeling.

3. GIANT TURTLES

At **Ranchos Las Primicias** and **Manzanillo**, you can find giant turtles in the wild. It is mandatory to visit with a guide.

The ranches are about 40 minutes from Puerto Ayora (**hours**: 7:00-18:00).

4. LAVA TUNNELS AND 'LOS GEMELOS'

The tunnels show "caves" of solidified lava. Los Gemelos are 2 volcanic craters where you can take a nice walk among the characteristic vegetation of the island.

5. LAS GRIETAS

Cracks in the **rock** where **seawater** enters. You can **dive** and **swim** among a great variety of fish. Natural light filters in creating a beautiful space.

6. PUERTO AYORA

Stroll around town among stores, **restaurants** and **bars** to get a taste of local life.

MUELLE DE LOS PESCADORES

San Cristobal *Island*

CERRO TIJERETAS
1. This **hill** is a perfect place for **hiking**. From the top you have good **views** of San Cristobal.

MUELLE TIJERETAS
2. Here you can **snorkel** for **free**. It is located near the town and the Tijeretas Hill. The waters at this point are crystal clear and there is great marine diversity.

GALAPAGUERA OF CERRO COLORADO
3. Perfect place in San Cristobal to see **giant turtles**. It is located 22 km (14 miles) **from Puerto Baquerizo** and can be reached by cab **in** only **40 minutes**.

360° TOUR
4. The **most popular tour** in San Cristobal: a boat takes you around the island in search of the most beautiful landscapes and is perfect for animal watching.

VISIT THE BEACHES
5. Some of the highlights are:

Playa Mann and **Punta Carola:** you can see many sea lions. You can walk there from the town.

Puerto Chino: the most beautiful beach according to many travelers to the island.

La Lobería: there you will find the largest number of sea lions. A 30-minute walk from downtown.

Isabela *Island*

1. CENTRO CRIANZA

This is a breeding and **protection center** for **giant tortoises** such as those on Santa Cruz and San Cristobal islands.

2. THE TUNNELS TOUR

The **most popular tour** on the island. It cannot be done in a day trip from Santa Cruz because of the tight travel times between islands. On this tour you can **snorkel** through **underwater caves** and **tunnels**. You can also see seahorses, turtles, small sharks and even penguins.

3. BLUE SHARKS TOUR

Another of Isabela's **most popular tours**. It can be done on a **round trip from Santa Cruz**. This tour takes you to see **penguins**, flamingos, sea lions, iguanas and **snorkel** among **blue sharks**.

4. SIERRA NEGRA VOLCANO

There is the possibility to **hike** to the top of the **volcano**. From there are fantastic **views** of the island.

5. CONCHA DE LA PERLA

A **bay** near the port where you can **swim** for free among sea lions, iguanas and if you are lucky, among penguins.

6. WALL FO TEARS

The wall was built by the prisoners of Isabela in the 20th century.

You can get there by bicycle and enjoy a **great view** from there.

THE TUNNELS

RANCHO LAS PRIMICIAS

What to do *Galapagos*

 Restaurants

1. **LA ISLA BONITA**
   (PUERTO AYORA) $-$$

2. **BAHÍA MAR**
   (PUERTO AYORA) $$

3. **MUY GALÁGOS**
   (PUERTO BAQUERIZO) $$

4. **PALM BEACH**
   (PUERTO VILLAMIL) $-$$

 Hotels

CACTUS HOTEL $$

Modern hotel located in the
heart of Puerto Baquerizo and
close to the airport.

GALAPAGOS MORNING
GLORY $$

Hotel located near the
beach, banks and stores
in Puerto Ayora.

Guayaquil

Restaurants | Large city

↑ **At this destination**

BEST TIME TO GO
JUNE-DECEMBER.

Guayaquil is **not** the most **popular** destination in Ecuador. **However**, there are some **interesting tourist spots** and **good connections**:

- **Most flights** to **Galapagos** stop or depart from Guayaquil.
- It is **3 hours** from **Montañita**.
- It is **3.5 hours** by bus from **Cuenca**.

You can also plan a good sightseeing tour with the recommendations of this guide.

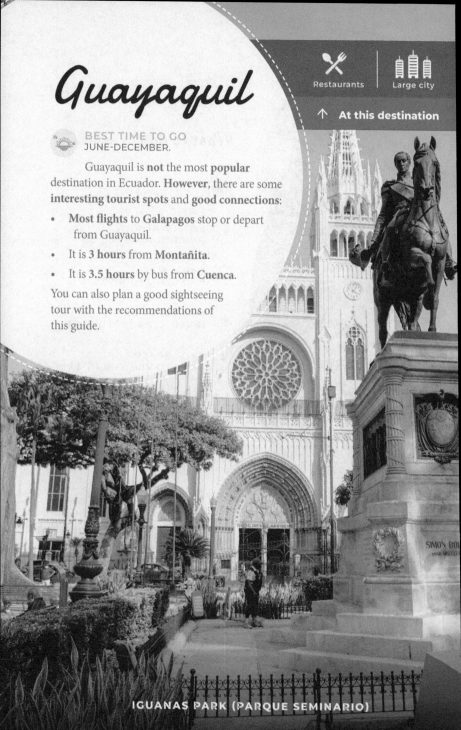

IGUANAS PARK (PARQUE SEMINARIO)

What to do *Guayaquil*

1. MALECÓN
This is a **walk** in an **urban park** along the Guayas River. Along the way you can find **bars, restaurants** and stores.

2. CABLECAR
A unique way to see Guayaquil going **over** the **river** and the city. It is a different way to see the city from another perspective.

3. IGUANAS PARK
The most **popular park** in Guayaquil and Ecuador. There you will find a multitude of **iguanas**. These animals are **not shy** and do not run away from humans.

'LAS PEÑAS' LIGHTHOUSE

IGUANAS PARK (PARQUE SEMINARIO)

4. SANTA ANA PORT
A **modern neighborhood** in Guayaquil with innovative architecture, marina, stores, **bars** and **restaurants**.

5. CHURUTE MANGROVES
A **natural reserve** only 45 minutes from Guayaquil. This natural reserve is home to a great variety of animal and plant species.

6. LAS PEÑAS
From the top of this neighborhood, you have an excellent **view** of the city and a famous **blue** and **white lighthouse**.

What to do *Guayaquil*

Restaurants

1. RIVIERA $$

2. LO NUESTRO $

3. MERCADO RÍO $

4. ODISEA BREWING $

Hotels

PEPE'S HOUSE GUAYAQUIL $$

Modern aparthotel located in a safe area of Guayaquil.

Montañita

Nightlife | Surfing | Beach

↑ **At this destination**

BEST TIME TO GO
MARCH-DECEMBER

Montañita is a town on the **coast** of the province of Santa Elena. It is known especially for its **nightlife** and **beach**.

Visitors can find a relaxed atmosphere perfect for relaxing and enjoying the sun and the sea. Although at night, the city transforms since it has a wide variety of **restaurants, bars** and nightclubs.

It is also a perfect place for **surfing** and other water activities.

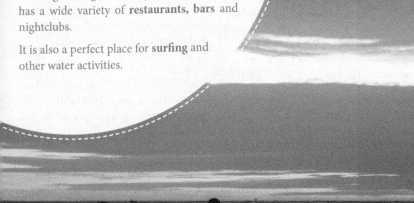

What to do *Montañita*

ENJOY THE BEACH
1. Montañita attracts national and international tourists because of its beach. There you can relax, **swim** and even eat at one of the many **ceviche** stands. Its **sunsets** are spectacular.

SURFING
2. It is a world-famous surfing destination. There you can easily find surf instructors and surfboard rentals.
There are good areas for **beginners** and **advanced** surfers.

NIGHLIFE
3. It has a great variety of **bars** and **discotheques**. There you can find one of the 25 best discos in the world: **Lost Beach**.

LOS FRAILES
4. It is a **Natural Park** with white sand **beaches** and crystal-clear waters near Montañita. There you can relax at Los Frailes, Playa Tortuguita and Playa Prieta beaches.

AYAMPE Y OLÓN
5. These are 2 beach destinations **near Montañita**, with **fewer people**, quieter, good beaches and **surf**.

ISLA DE LA PLATA
6. Known as the 'Galapagos of the poor'. You can get there by tour and see a great variety of birds and marine species.

The excursions cost between **$35-45**. They depart around 9:30 am **from Puerto López**.

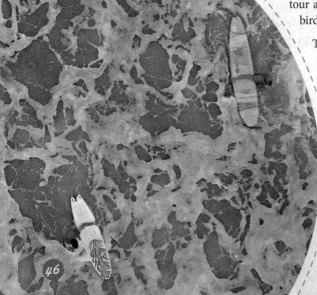

What to do *Montañita*

 *Restaurants*

1. SHANKHA SUSHI N' THAI $-$$

3. SHAWARMA ARABE $

2. TAMBO SABORES PERUANOS $

4 MEDIAS DULCES $

 Hotels

CASA DEL SOL

$$

Hostel located in a quiet area. It usually has yoga classes, surfing and a perfect balance between travelers who want to have fun

Cuenca

BEST TIME TO GO
MAY-SEPTEMBER

Cuenca is for many tourists, the most beautiful city in Ecuador. It is located in the **south** of the country, about 3 hours from Guayaquil and Baños.

On your visit to Cuenca, you can explore its museums, art galleries and tour the city center. There you can climb to the top of the **cathedral** and stroll through its **picturesque streets** and **squares**.

CUENCA CATHEDRAL

What to do *Cuenca*

1. CAJAS NATIONAL PARK
In Cajas National Park you can do one of the best **hikes** in Ecuador.

Although it is **4,000 meters** (13,000 ft) above sea level, it is not a technical hike and is suitable for **all types** of **hikers**.

It is about **45 minutes** by **bus** from **Cuenca** and is totally free.

2. TURI VIEWPOINT
From here, you can get a **scenic view** of **Cuenca** and spectacular landscapes.

3. CLIMB THE CATHEDRAL
The visit to the **top** of the **cathedral** of the Immaculate Conception costs $2.

From the top, you have beautiful **views** of the cathedral domes and the city.

4. HISTORICAL CENTER
The historic center of Cuenca is a **World Heritage Site**.

If you stroll through its streets, you can enjoy its **colonial architecture**, old churches, squares and cobblestone streets.

5. LOCAL GASTRONOMY
Don't leave Cuenca without trying **locro** (potato soup with avocado, avocado, aguardiente and meat or chicken), **hornado** (roast pork), **seco** (dried beef dish) and empanadas de verde (filled with potato and spinach).

One of the best places to try these dishes is the '**10 de Agosto**' **market**.

CAJAS NATIONAL PARK

What to do *Cuenca*

 Restaurants

1. MERCADO
'10 DE AGOSTO' $

2. TIESTO'S CAFE
RESTAURANT $$

3. EL MERCADO $$

4 MANGIARE BENNE $$

Hotels

POSADA TODOS SANTOS
$$

Cozy hotel located in the historic
center of Cuenca.

 Prices

$ = UP TO $15
$$ = $15-50
$$$ = FROM $50

'10 DE AGOSTO'
MARKET

Baños

BEST TIME TO GO
MAY-SEPTEMBER

Baños is another of the most **adventurous** destinations in Ecuador. The small town is surrounded by steep and **high mountains**.

It is located about **5 hours** from **Cuenca** and **3 hours** from **Quito**. Very close to the 5,000 meters (16,400 ft) high active volcano called Tungurahua.

Baños is famous for its natural beauty and **adventure sports**, such as rafting, biking and hiking.

PAILÓN DEL DIABLO

What to do *Baños*

1. **BIKE RIDE**
You can take a nice ride through the town of Baños. You will go through beautiful landscapes between **mountains** and **waterfalls**. This activity is recommended even for beginners.

2. **PAILÓN DEL DIABLO**
A beautiful waterfall more than **30 meters (100 ft) high**. This causes impressive clouds of water vapor. The tour is between suspension bridges and a cobblestone road.

3. **HOT SPRINGS**
These are **pools** of **naturally heated water**. They are located at the foot of the **waterfall** of the **Virgin**.

4. **VIEWPOINT**
You can get there on a **little train** that leaves from the center of the village. You have incredible **views** of the town and the **Tungurahua volcano**.

5. **ADVENTURE**
Baños, known as the 'portal of adventures': it offers **rafting**, bungee jumping and **mountain biking** activities.

6. **AMAZON**
From Baños take an excursion to **Puyo**. It is the **gateway** to the **Amazon**.

What to do *Baños*

Restaurants

1. JAGUAR
HOUSE $

2. SWISS
BISTRO $-$$

Hotels

ERUPTION ART HOTEL $

Hostel with fantastic views,
restaurant and private bar.
Located in the center of
Baños.

WATERFALLS
AT PAILÓN DEL
DIABLO

Cotopaxi

BEST TIME TO GO
FEBRUARY-MAY

Cotopaxi is possibly the **most famous volcano** in **Ecuador** because it is a beautiful and **perfect volcanic cone**. It is the second highest peak in the country (5,897 meters/19,347 ft).

It is a popular destination for **nature** and **mountain lovers**. In Cotopaxi National Park, there are cabins and hostels where you can stay. There you can enjoy a wide range of activities such as **hiking, mountaineering**, climbing and horseback riding.

Nature | Hiking

↑ **At this destination**

What to do *Cotopaxi*

HIKING

1. In **Cotopaxi National Park** there are several **trails** for all types of **hikers** from easy to advance level.

It is a very good way to experience nature in another ecosystem of Ecuador. You can learn more about the biodiversity and geology of the region.

MOUNTAINEERING

2. This is a very **physically demanding adventure** in which you must have previously acclimatized to in order to minimize altitude sickness. It is essential that you hire a mountain guide or agency.

FLORA AND FAUNA

3. In the Cotopaxi Park, you can hopefully see deers, Andean foxes, páramo birds such as the Andean condor, marmots and vicuñas.

In addition, the walks will be among **lagoons** and typical cloud forest, páramo and **Andean forest vegetation**.

HORSE RIDING

4. Another way to see the landscapes of the National Park.

This way, you can enjoy the views in a quieter and more restful way.

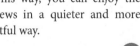

CHUQUIRAGUA FLOWER

What to do *Cotopaxi*

 Restaurants

1. MIRADOR DE LOS VOLCANES $

2. RONDADOR COTOPAXI $

3. CHASQUI MIRADOR COTOPAXI $

Climbing agencies / Guides

1. CUMBRE TOURS

2. NANUK ADVENTURES

3. LENIN LÓPEZ (INSTAGRAM: @LENCLIMB9)

4. NICO NAVARRETE (INSTAGRAM: @NICOLAS_NAVARRETE.EC)

COTOPAXI SUMMIT

Amazon

BEST TIME TO GO
AUGUST-FEBRUARY

The **4 most common destinations** to **visit** the **Amazon** in Ecuador are:
PUYO |TENA | YASUNÍ | CUYABENO

During **my visit** to Ecuador, I chose to visit the **Cuyabeno** area. While **Puyo** and **Tena** are at the **gates** of the **Amazon, Yasuni** and **Cuyabeno are further inland** in the **jungle**. This allows **more animals** to be seen and the experience to be more authentic. In addition, **Cuyabeno** is **cheaper than Yasuní** (300 Vs 1,000 dollars on average).

What to do
Amazon

HIKING
1. The hikes are always done with a **tour guide**. He will tell you about the properties of the flora and fauna you encounter.

NIGHT WALK
2. The jungle is full of life at night. Especially **spiders, scorpions,** other **insects** and **snakes**. Walking in the dark in search of them is exciting.

BOAT RIDE
3. It is the most comfortable and **fastest way** to **see birds, monkeys** and explore the Amazon landscapes. There are also **night boat** rides, where you will see dozens of **caimans** and even tree boas.

ANIMALS
4. You can encounter many **birds, monkeys, snakes, caimans** and thousands of **insects**. Although it is more complicated, there is the possibility of seeing **anacondas**.

INDIGENOUS COMMUNITY
5. Indigenous communities still live in the Ecuadorian Amazon. Some of them can be visited and **collaborate** with **tourist activities**.

BATHE IN A LAKE
6 Excursions in the Cuyabeno Amazon usually end with a swim in a lake. They are done at **sunset**, so the baths at that point are movie-like. Caimans are not active at that point of the day. Therefore, there is no risk for tourists.

What to do *Amazon*

Agencies (Tours)

 Hotels

1. IMAGINE ECUADOR

2. PAPANGU TOURS

3. COMUNITY ADVENTURES ECUADOR

CUYABENO RIVER LODGE

$$$

Lodging in cabins in the
middle of the Amazon.

Mindo

 BEST TIME TO GO
MAY-SEPTEMBER

Mindo is a small town in the Andes region of Ecuador. It stands out for its **nature**: walks through **cloud forests**, rafting on rivers and visits to **waterfalls** and lagoons. It is also a special destination for **bird** and **butterfly watching**.

Finally, it is a perfect location for those looking for **tranquility**, a good gastronomic offer and to buy and taste the best **chocolate** and **coffee** in the country.

BUTTERFLY GARDEN

What to do
Mindo

1. TUBING
Take a float down the Mindo River. **Rafting** is also popular in this location.

2. BUTTERFLIES OF MINDO
There are **2 butterfly gardens** in Mindo: Mariposario Nathaly Mindo and Mariposas de Mindo.

The second one is the most impressive. It is located 2 km (1.2 miles) from the town. There you can walk among beautiful species of butterflies.

3. WATERFALLS
Mindo is in the middle of nature. One of its best activities is hiking to waterfalls: 'Cascadas del amor' and 'Cascada de Nambillo'.

4. BIRDWATCHING
Mindo is a paradise for **bird lovers**. This destination has about **550** different **species**.

5. TARABITA
This is a **cable car**. It transports you **above** the **forest** and takes you to the entrance of the **"waterfall sanctuary"**. The experience is worth it for the excellent views.

6. CHOCOLATE/COFFEE
Mindo is also known for its **chocolate** and **coffee production**. There you can learn about the elaborate production process and taste them.

What to do *Mindo*

 Restaurants

1. **EL QUETZAL (CHOCOLATE TOUR)**

2. **MINROOT RESTAURANTE $**

3. **BIO MINDO $**

4. **MINDO FOREST COFFE&TEA $**

5. **THE FOOD STUDIO $$**

Hotels

MINDO REAL $

Nice hotel with swimming pool in the middle of nature and 5 minutes from downtown.

Galapagos
Guide

1. Islands
in Galapagos

- Galapagos is made up of **13 large islands**, 9 small islands and 107 rocks jutting out of the sea.
- They are located **1,300 km** (800 miles) **west** of Ecuador, in the Pacific Ocean.
- They are very **active volcanic islands**, especially Isabela and Fernandina.

Santa Cruz

1. The **best island** to see **giant tortoises** in the wild. You can see them at El Rancho Las Primicias and Rancho El Chato.

2. The island with the best connections, **hotels** and bars.

3. It does **not** have the **greatest diversity** of animal species, but it has many points of interest to visit.

4. It has an **airport**.

5. It is the **most populated** and touristic island.

6. Tourists stay on this island in **Puerto Ayora**.

GALAPAGOS ISLANDS

San Cristóbal

1. Its most important city is **Puerto Baquerizo**.

2. The **second most populated**.

3. It has an **airport**.

4. With **spectacular beaches** and perfect to see sea lions.

Isabela

1. The **largest island**. Visitors stay in **Puerto Villamil**.

2. You can find blue footed boobies, sea turtles and **penguins** (they can only be seen in 2 islands).

3. It has several spectacular areas for **snorkeling**.

4. The **third in population** (2300 inhabitants).

Española

1. It is **not inhabited**.

2. The island with **more land animals** per **square meter**, especially iguanas and a large number of sea lions.

3. The island with the **largest** number and **variety** of **birds**.

Floreana

1. It has a **population** of just over **100 people**.

2. One of the **most biodiverse**, both terrestrial and marine.

3. It has probably the **best snorkeling** in Galapagos: sea turtles, sharks, rays, sea lions and hundreds of fish.

2. **Three**
options

3 ways to visit Galapagos islands

1. BY YOURSELF

• **Advantages:**
1) It is the most economical.

2) Total freedom of schedules and choice of activities.

• **Disadvantages**:
1) May be more difficult to see certain animals.

2) Transportation on your own by foot, bicycle, cab or ferry.

2. TOURS

• **Advantages:**
1) It's a convenient option, since you don't have to worry about transportation or planning.

2) They will show you the most interesting places.

• **Disadvantages**:
1) It is not a cheap option. Tours usually cost from $140 and up.

2) There are some very commercial tours. They usually show you a lot of spots in one day and you are not free to stay in one place even if you are comfortable.

3. CRUISE

• **Advantages:**
1) Convenient option since the route is planned. You sleep and eat on the ship; you don't have to worry about finding restaurants and hotels.

2) It is the way you will see more animals and islands.

• **Disadvantages**:
1) It is the most expensive option.
2) Little freedom to explore on your own or visit local life on the islands.

🚌 *Transportation*

1. AIRPORTS

Tourists enter the islands through these **2 airports**:

- **San Cristobal** city airport: the airport is only a 15-minute walk (or 2-minute cab ride) from the town of Puerto Baquerizo.

- **Galapagos Seymour** Ecological Airport: located on the island of **Baltra**. It is the airport that **connects** to the island of **Santa Cruz**, since both islands are separated by only a few meters.

2. FLIGHTS

Read this information carefully about flights to Galapagos:

- There are **only direct flights** to Galapagos from **Quito** (2 h 20 min) and the vast majority, from **Guayaquil** (1 h. 50 minutes).
- Flights depart **between 8:00 am** and **12:30 pm**.
- Prices range from **$190-600**.
- At the **entrance** you are asked to see your **return ticket** (maximum stay allowed is 2 months).

- **Emetebe** and **Flygalapagos** airlines offer **internal flights** between Isabela, Santa Cruz and San Cristobal islands. They cost around $130 and have a duration of 30 minutes.

Transportation

👀 FERRY ITINERARIES:

Transportation between islands is usually done by **small boats**. There are only ferries **between these islands**:

- Isabela-Santa Cruz
- Santa Cruz-San Cristóbal
- Santa Cruz-Floreana (only Tuesdays and Thursdays)

📍 FERRY INFORMATION

- The price of a **one-way ticket** is **$30-35**.
- Try to **buy** your ticket **2 days** in **advance** as there is limited availability. You can buy them in any of the agencies in the cities of Galapagos.

📅 Ferry

OUTGOING: 7 AM (APROX.)
RETURN: 3 PM (APROX.)

RANCHO LAS PRIMICIAS

3. Cruise
Galapagos

STARTING POINT

- Most cruises **depart** from Baltra Island or San Cristobal Island (**from the airports**). Some also depart from Puerto Ayora.
- The cruise ship will pick you up from the airport and take you to the ship.

CRUISE LENGTH:

- The Galapagos cruises are classified as **4 days**, 5 days and 8 days. But in reality, they **translate into 2,** 3 and 6 **full days**.
- The **first** and **last day** of the Galapagos cruise are **short days** (they begin and end with the arrival and departure of the flight between 09:30 and 11:30).
- The **shortest cruises last 4 days** and the **longest** cruises last **15** days.

RECOMMENDED DURATION:

- **5 days**: during this time, you see the essentials in Galapagos (species and points of the most important islands).
- **7 days**: if you want to explore the islands in more depth.

ITINERARIO

- **Most boats visit similar sites**: Baltra airport, Santa Cruz Island, Española, Floreana, North Seymour, Santa Fe and San Cristobal.

- The **less visited** but **recommended** islands are **Fernandina, Isabela** and **Genovesa**.
- The trips **between islands** are made at **night**.

$ PRICES

- The approximate **cost** of a 5-day cruise in Galapagos is **$2,000**.
- **Recommendation**: quote the price of **last-minute trips**. The price can be reduced by **up to half** (there are last-minute cancellations, and the agencies are looking to sell those tickets).

TO KEEP IN MIND

- On a cruise you can observe a greater number of species of fauna and flora.
- All **meals** are **included**.
- **All activities** (snorkeling, kayaking, paddleboarding, etc.) are **included**.
- There is a bilingual **naturalist guide**.

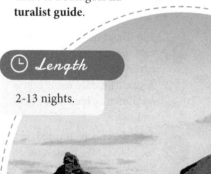

⏱ Length

2-13 nights.

Tips

1. The **island most prepared** for **tourism** is **Santa Cruz** Island, in the city of Puerto Ayora. There are many hotels, restaurants, pharmacies, bars and tours.

2. **Internet** is quite **limited** on the islands. The hostels usually have Wi-Fi, but it is slow and gets cut off. The same happens with telephone **data**. The company with the **best signal** is **Claro**.

3. There are only **ATMs** on **Santa Cruz** and **San Cristobal islands**.

4. Take **hydrodramine** for the ferry ride between islands. It will help with the **motion sickness** of going by **boat**.

5. Flights usually appear **cheaper** if you go to the Avianca and Latam airlines pages on the **Ecuadorian sites**.

Tourist taxes

Travel to the Galapagos Islands is **expensive**. These are some of the tourist **fees** and expenses on your visit:

1. Entrance fee: **$100** for **foreign** citizens over 12 years old. It is **paid upon arrival** at the **island**. The fee for children under 12 is $3 and for Ecuadorians $6.

2. Transit control card: **$20**. You must buy it near the check-in area (before the security checkpoint) at the **airport** in Quito or Guayaquil.

3. **Isabela** Island charges an entrance fee of **$10**.

4. To enter each island by ferry, you have to pay $2: **one dollar** for the **boat-taxi** (ferries do not go to the dock) and **one dollar** for the dock **occupancy fee**.

Unique
Experiences

1. Be around *animals*

The islands are home to a large number of **endemic species** found nowhere else in the world. Among them are the iconic giant tortoises, iguanas and sea lions.

These animals are known to be **unafraid** of **humans** and very curious. Therefore, tourists can relax on the beach or even in the city and be surrounded by these animals.

The preservation of all these species is a priority for the islands. So as a tourist, you can rest assured that the money from tourism is largely dedicated to preserving the ecosystem.

SANTA CRUZ STREETS

◎ GALAPAGOS

Closest point
to the sun

2.

Chimborazo is the **highest mountain** on the planet if **measured** from the **center** of the **earth**. Planet earth, not being totally spherical, is closer to the atmosphere from the equator.

Mount Chimborazo is located just one degree south of the equator. It rises **6,268 meters** (20,560 ft) above sea level, making it the highest peak in the country.

The ascent is one of the most difficult in the Ecuadorian Andes, due to the reduced oxygen at the summit, physical hardship and changing weather conditions. Therefore, it is mandatory to make the ascent with an experienced guide and equipment.

 FROM $500

 MOUNT
CHIMBORAZO

$25/CLASS

MONTAÑITA

3.

Surfing in
Montañita

Montañita is one of the most popular destinations for surfers in Ecuador. It has consistent and **strong waves**, **warm weather** and a vibrant atmosphere. In addition, the beaches of Montañita are wide and perfect for relaxing on the beach.

In Montañita there are waves for all levels. So more experienced surfers or beginners can enjoy the waves. There are several surf schools and rental stores in the area.

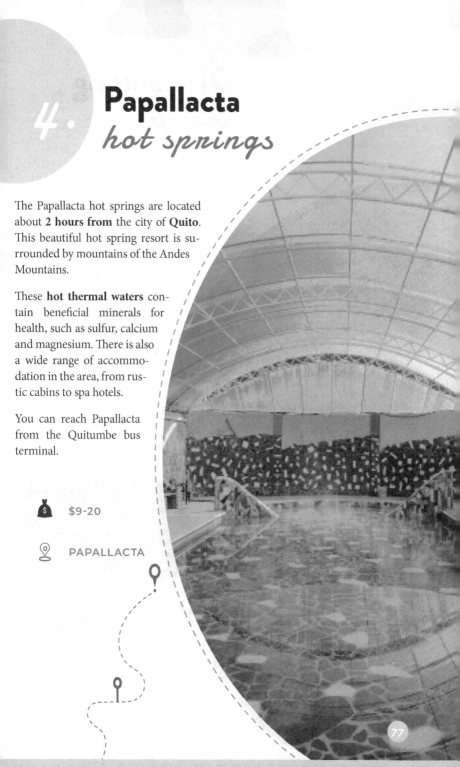

4. Papallacta
hot springs

The Papallacta hot springs are located about **2 hours from** the city of **Quito**. This beautiful hot spring resort is surrounded by mountains of the Andes Mountains.

These **hot thermal waters** contain beneficial minerals for health, such as sulfur, calcium and magnesium. There is also a wide range of accommodation in the area, from rustic cabins to spa hotels.

You can reach Papallacta from the Quitumbe bus terminal.

$9-20

PAPALLACTA

5. Dive among *sharks*

Hammerhead sharks are one of the most emblematic species of Galapagos. They can be found in large groups at certain times of the year. Diving with these animals is one of the best experiences in Ecuador if you know how to dive.

In addition, from **June to September** you can also see **humpback whales**. It is common to see them from boats, diving and even jumping out of the water.

$180 /2 DIVES

GALAPAGOS

6.
Bath in a lake
Amazon

Ecuador offers the possibility to explore one of the most biodiverse areas in the world: the Amazon region. The Amazonian areas of Cuyabeno and Yasuní are home to a great variety of animals: caimans, anacondas, monkeys or toucans.

Tour activities usually include **jungle hikes, boat rides** and **animal searches**.

One of the star activities is the **sunsets** from the lakes. Travelers can also **swim** in the **lake**. Although caimans live there, they do not pose a threat since they are not active at that time of day.

 FROM $300

 CUYABENO/YASUNÍ

Visit the indigenous market in *Otavalo*

7.

The Otavalo market is one of the largest **indigenous** handicraft **markets** in Latin America. Although it is held every day, **Saturdays** are the **busiest** days for visitors and vendors.

In the market you can buy **textiles, ceramics, jewelry** and wooden objects among others. You can also find local food stalls.

Otavalo is located **2 hours** by bus (Terminal Terrestre de Carcelén) **from Quito**.

 $6 (BUS)

 OTAVALO

Middle of the world *Museum*

8.

The **Intiñán museum** is an opportunity to explore the **equatorial line** and learn about the history and culture of the region.

The museum is located on the Equator, which divides the world into 2 hemispheres.

Among the various **scientific experiments**, you can experience the zero gravity of the equator and observe how water rotates in different directions in the two hemispheres (Coriolis effect).

 $5

 QUITO

Best in Ecuador

Mountaineering and hiking

These are the 6 best hiking and mountainee-ring routes in Ecuador.

Best in Ecuador:
mountaineering/hiking

EL ALTAR

1. It is one of the **most beautiful hikes** in Ecuador. The adventure usually lasts 2 days and aims to reach the beautiful **turquoise water lagoon**. On the other hand, the ascent to the summit (5,319 meters/ 17,450 ft) of El Altar is very technical that few hikers usually do.

 WHERE
Riobamba

 DIFFICULTY
Middle-low

QUILOTOA

2. The Quilotoa hike (**Quilotoa Loop**) lasts **3-5 days**. It runs through several Andean villages around the Quilotoa Lagoon. It offers panoramic views of rivers, mountains and valleys among indigenous communities.

Good option for those looking to hike in Ecuador, without having to hike high peaks. It never reaches than 3,000 m./9,800 ft.

Many travelers prefer to **make a day trip** from Quito and just **observe** the beauty of the **lagoon**.

 **WHERE**
4 h. from Quito

DIFFICULTY
Low

Best in Ecuador:
mountaineering/hiking

3. RUCU PICHINCHA

It is located **next** to **Quito**. You can get there by cab and then by cable car.

From the top of the **cable car** (4,000 meters/ 13,120 ft), you can **start** the **hike** to the summit of Rucu Pichincha (4,776 meters/ 15,700 ft). The last part of the ascent is harder than a simple hike and requires you to be well-equipped.

WHERE
Quito

DIFFICULTY
Medium-low

4. PARQUE CAJAS

Cajas National Park has more than **200 lakes**, surrounded by imposing mountains, paramo landscapes and **cloud forests**.

Entrance is **free** and there are trails of varying difficulty and duration. Be careful with the altitude since walking between 3,000 m. (9,843 ft)-4,000 m. (13,123 ft) isn't easy.

WHERE
Cuenca

DIFFICULTY
Low

Best in Ecuador:
mountaineering/hiking

5. COTOPAXI

It is one of the highest active volcanoes in the world with 5,897 meters/17,350 ft (second summit of Ecuador). There are **2 options**: **hiking** through the natural park, enjoying the landscapes, flora, fauna and incredible views. **Or** the more daring, who choose to **climb** to the **summit** of this majestic volcano.

WHERE
45 km Quito

DIFFICULTY
Medium-high

6. CHIMBORAZO

The **highest peak** in **Ecuador** at 6,263 meters/20,500 ft. There is the option of hiking in a more relaxed way or mountaineering for the more experienced.

If you choose to climb to the summit, you have to complete several peaks before to get used to the altitude. It is also essential to be physically strong and to go with an **experienced guide**. The agency '**Nanuk adventures**" organizes trips to Chimborazo.

WHERE
150 km from Quito

DIFFICULTY
High

Wildlife

Ecuador has an unparalleled diversity due to its ecosystems: you can find from giant tortoises in the Galapagos to whales in the Pacific, bears and llamas in the Andes and jaguars or caimans in the Amazon.

Best in Ecuador:
Wildlife

1. SEA LIONS

The Galapagos sea lion is a carnivorous mammal species. It only inhabits the Galapagos Islands.

The population is about 50,000 specimens.

It is one of the star animals in the islands: they can be found in the **streets** of the island of **Santa Cruz**. In addition, they are usually not very shy and coexist on the beach and dive among humans.

📍 **WHERE**
Galapagos

2. GIANT TORTOISES

These tortoises can **only** be seen in the **Seychelles** and **Galapagos** islands.

They can **live up to 175 years**, weigh up to 300 kg (600 lb), measure up to 1.5 meters (5 ft) and are herbivorous.

📍 **WHERE**
Galapagos

Best in Ecuador:
Wildlife

3. IGUANAS

Galapagos has **4 species** of **iguanas**:

- **Marine**: endemic species (has a diving capacity of 60 minutes).
- **Pale land** iguana: only on Santa Fe Island.
- **Yellow land** iguana.
- **Pink**: discovered in 2009. It lives only on the summit of Wolf volcano on Isabela.

📍 **WHERE**
Galapagos

4. BIRDS

Ecuador is a world power in the preservation of birds: it has **1,640 species** of the 9,700 worldwide (third country in the world with more birds).

The great variety stands out, since the species are different in the Galapagos Islands, on the Pacific coast, in the Andes and Amazon.

Some of the most famous are the blue-footed booby, the red-footed booby, masked booby and the royal frigate birds.

📍 **WHERE**
Ecuador

Best in Ecuador:
Wildlife

5. PINK DOLPHIN

Ecuador's Amazon is home to a great variety of animals: otters, jaguars, anacondas, tarantulas, scorpions and caimans.

One of the star animals that you can easily see is the river dolphin. The largest species of **river dolphin** lives there and some of them have a **pink color**.

⦿ WHERE
Amazon

6. LLAMAS

In Ecuador you can find **llamas, vicuñas** or **alpacas**. All three belong to the South American camelid family.

They can be found in the **highland regions**.

⦿ WHERE
Chimborazo/
Cotopaxi

Transportation

These are the main means of transportation in Ecuador: bus, cab, boat and air transportation. In this section about transportation, you can read about its:

**TRANSPORT SPEED | COST
SAFETY | EASE OF USE**

Transportation *Ecuador*

LONG DISTANCE

- Transportation in Ecuador is usually by **plane** or **bus**.

- **Roads** are of **good quality** compared to other neighboring countries.

- It is only about **8 hours by bus** from **Quito to Guayaquil** or **Cuenca**.

- There are **round-trip flights** from $60 between **domestic** destinations.

- Ecuador does **not** have efficient **train routes** connecting the major cities or destinations I recommend.

 AIRLINES

Flying is **not** an **essential** transportation option in Ecuador (there are only 8 hours by bus between Quito and Guayaquil/Cuenca).

The **only exception** is if you travel to the **Galapagos** Islands. Going by plane is the only way to get there.

To book transportation in Ecuador, the best option is 12toGo.

On this platform you can find all the routes and means of transportation in Ecuador. In addition, the page shows you a comparison of prices and number of hours between the different destinations.

THESE ARE THE 2 MAIN AIRLINES IN ECUADOR:

- Avianca
- Latam

ALL THESE DESTINATIONS HAVE AN AIRPORT:

- **Galapagos**: Santa Cruz Island (Seymour airport on Santa Cruz Island and San Cristobal airport).
- **Guayaquil**
- **Cuenca**
- **Quito**

Tip
Remember to take care of your belongings during the the bus ride. Thefts are common.

Transportation *Ecuador*

BUS

Going by bus is one of the **best ways** to **travel** around Ecuador. The distances are not long, and it is inexpensive: an **8-hour ride** from Guayaquil to Quito costs about **$20**.

Except for the **night buses**, **many** of them are **old** and tend to drive too **fast**. The easiest way to book a bus is at the terminal itself. Buses usually **leave every hour** and there is **no need** to **book** in **advance**.

On this **website** you can find more **information** about bus terminals and bus companies in Ecuador:

https://www.ecuadorbus.com.ec/

1. Quito (Terminal Quitumbe)

- **Guayaquil (Terminal terrestre de Guayaquil):**
- Flota Imbabura.
- Transportes Ecuador.
- Transportes Panamericana.

2. Quito (Terminal Quitumbe)- Baños (Terminal Terrestre de Baños):

- Baños Cooperativa De Transportes y Turismo.
- Expreso Baños.
- Flota Pelileo.
- Amazonas Cooperativa de Transportes.

3. Quito (Terminal Quitumbe)-Cuenca (Terminal Terrestre de Cuenca):

- Flota Imbabura.
- Cooperativa Patria.
- Unión Cariamanga Internacional.
- Panamericana.
- Super Taxis.

4. Guayaquil (Terminal terrestre de Guayaquil)- Montañita:

- Baños Cooperativa de Transportes y Turismo.
- Cooperativa Libertad Peninsular.
- CITUP Cooperativa de Transporte Unidos Peninsulares.

Transportation *Ecuador*

CAR RENTAL

Renting a car is also a **popular option** for tourists to Ecuador:

- Renting costs about **$56** on average.
- On average it is **$225** if you rent it for a **week** ($32/day).
- **Roads** are **well maintained** and paved.
- There are a multitude of $1 tolls.

- You must be **21 years old** to rent a car.
- You only need your country's license and passport to rent.
- The **maximum speed** on the highway is **100 km/h** (62 mil/h).
- You drive in the **right lane**.

BOAT

In Ecuador you can enjoy boat transportation in the Galapagos Islands. There are 2 different ways:

- Transportation with boats **between** the **Galapagos islands**.
- **Cruise** in Galapagos.

Transportation *Ecuador*

IN THE BIG CITIES

- **Uber only** works in **Quito** and **Guayaquil** among the cities I recommend. It is the safe, fast and affordable way to transport yourself on your own.

- **Besides Uber**, there are other cab ordering apps, such as **Didi** or **InDriver**.

- Although it is possible to order cabs on the street, it is **safer** if: A) You ask the **hotel** for a **safe cab**; B) You order a cab using an **app**.

- **Quito** has a **metro line** that was inaugurated at the end of 2022. It runs through the city from north to south. The ticket costs $0.45.

- **Quito** and **Guayaquil** also have an **extensive bus network**. Although it is **slower** transport, it is not as safe and complicated to understand.

TAXI TAXI FROM AIRPORTS

- **Quito:** $25 (40 minutes). Uber? Yes.

- **Guayaquil:** airport in the heart of the city center. Uber? Yes.

- **Cuenca:** $4 (8 min). Uber? No.

- **Santa Cruz:** $11-36 (1.5 h). Uber? No.

- **San Cristobal:** $4 (4 min.) Uber? No.

CUENCA

Essential to
Know

Currency and costs

The **cost** of traveling to Ecuador is **mid-range** compared to other Latin American countries. One of the reasons is that Ecuador uses a strong currency (the dollar):

- **Cheaper than** Costa Rica, Brazil, Chile, Mexico, Panama or Uruguay.
- **More expensive than** Colombia, Argentina or Bolivia.

CURRENCY

There are **2 ways** to **get dollars** in Ecuador:

1. ATM'S

Compare the **commissions** when withdrawing money since the difference can be large between different ATMs.

2. EXCHANGE HOUSES

In **Quito, Guayaquil, Cuenca** and **airports** you can find exchange houses.

CREDIT/DEBIT CARDS

Payment by **debit** or **credit card** in Ecuador is quite **common**. Especially in urban areas. Restaurants, hotels and most establishments accept cards.

Visa and **Mastercard** are **commonly accepted**. **American Express** is **not as common**.

However, I **do not recommend traveling without cash**. In smaller establishments or in less populated areas, you cannot pay by card.

It is also common for **some establishments** to charge a **surcharge** when using a **card**. So, it may be cheaper to pay the fee when withdrawing money at ATMs.

TIPPING

Tipping is **not part** of the **culture** in Ecuador. However, there are **exceptions**:

- In **fancier restaurants**: 10-15%.
- **Tour guides**: $10-20.
- On **Galapagos cruises**: $20 to the guide and $15 to the crew per day.

Where tipping is NOT expected:

- In the most basic restaurants or cafes.
- In cabs.

Please note that in restaurants 10% of the service is already included. Even so, there are customers who choose to tip.

COST OF FOOD AND DRINKS

Eating in restaurants can cost the following **prices**:

- Small **traditional restaurant**: $3-5.
- **Mid-range** restaurant: $10-15
- **Fancy** restaurants: starting at $50 for 2 people.

These are the **average prices** for some items:

- **Local beer** (0.5 L): $2.5
- **Coffee** $2.30
- **Water bottle** (0.33 L): $0.60
- **Ticket in local transportation**: $0.35.

Currency *and costs*

ATM

In Ecuador there are **ATMs** in **most destinations**:

- In big cities.
- Towns.
- Galapagos: on the islands of San Cristobal and Santa Cruz.
- You can find ATMs in shopping malls, supermarkets, airports and bus stations.
- If you go to the **Amazon**, I recommend that you **carry cash**.

Tip
Before the trip starts, take into account costs such as airfare or travel insurance.

TRANSPORTATION COSTS

- **Bus:** bus fares between cities can range from **$4 to $20**.
- **Plane:** you can find flights between Quito, Guayaquil and Cuenca from **$30**.

- **Galapagos flights**: flying to Galapagos is **more expensive**. If you find a **good deal**, the price is **$190** (round trip). Although the most common is to pay $400 minimum for round trip tickets.

PRICE IN DOLLARS	LOW BUDGET	MEDIUM	HIGH BUDGET
Hotels	10	40	100
Food	10	25	90
Transportation	5	10	25
Tickets	5	20	30
TOTAL	$30	$95	$245

Currency *and costs*

Traveling in Ecuador can be even more economical if you follow these **tips**:

1. Take money out in large amounts. **Avoid** continuous **ATM fees**.

2. **Travel** by **bus** between cities. Ecuador is not a giant country. The maximum time between cities is 8 hours.

3. Try to **negotiate prices** in **markets** when buying handicrafts or gifts and compare the price of tours.

4. If you take a **Galapagos cruise**, **book** a **last minute** one: you can save almost half the price (from $2,200 to $1,200).

5. In **Galapagos**, local restaurants offer **lunch (almuerzos)** for **$5** (international restaurants start at $15).

6. **Eat** at **markets**. Typical food or "lunch" usually costs between **$3-5**.

7. Try to do **activities** on your own **for free** in **Galapagos**. Tours are expensive and often offer activities that you can actually do **without** a **guide**.

Hotels

Booking a hotel on your trip to Ecuador is very easy. You can find accommodation for **all budgets**. If you are traveling without a lot of money, you can book accommodation in hostels or hotels which offer beds in shared rooms or private rooms for very little money.

If, on the other hand, you prefer a more comfortable place with privacy, you can book a room in a more **luxurious** hotel for as little as **$100**.

BOOK ONLINE

Booking a hostel or hotel is very easy and the best way to travel in Ecuador. You can book several nights in a row and in most cases, you can cancel your stay in case something unexpected happens.

Except for important **holidays** (such as Christmas) **or** in **Galapagos**, you **can book** on **short notice**. Ecuador has a wide variety of accommodation and there is no mass tourism.

HOTEL/RESORT

The destinations I tell you about in Ecuador are very touristic. Therefore, you will find hotels for all budgets:

Warning
Do not confuse Cuenca (Ecuador) with Cuenca (Spain). Many travelers mistakenly book hotels in Cuenca, Spain, as it often appears as the top search result. It's important to note that there is a city with the same name in Spain.

Hotels

- The **average price** for **budget** hotels is around **$29**.
- **Mid-range** hotels cost about **$50**.
- **5-star** hotels can be booked starting at **$100**.

HOSTELS

This is the **cheapest** way to stay in Ecuador:

- You can find a bed in a shared room **from $8**.

- If you prefer to have a **private** room, prices start at **$18**.
- If you are traveling alone and want to **meet travelers**, this is the **best option** to stay.

AIRBNB

In **all destinations** in Ecuador, you can find accommodation through **Airbnb**:

- Prices for apartments range **from $20**.
- I recommend accommodation in **mountainous** areas. There are **cabins** in spectacular landscapes.

Culture

Ecuador has a rich and **diverse culture**. It spans from **pre-Hispanic cultures**, from **colonial** times to the present. Each **region** (coast, Galapagos, highlands and Amazon) has its **own traditions** and customs.

DO'S	DON'TS
Keep a distance of **2 meters** *from the* **animals in Galapagos**.	*Wear clothes that do not* **cover your knees** *and* **shoulders** *in churches.*
Ask permission *when taking* **pictures** *of* **people**, *especially members of indigenous communities.*	**Do not expect activities** *to happen in a* **timely manner**. *Especially parties or social events.*
Greet people *with a high-five, hug or kiss on the cheek.*	**Don't accept** *the* **first price** *at* **markets**. *It is common for them to raise prices when they detect that you are a foreigner.*
Say **'que aproveche'** *(enjoy your meal) before eating.*	**Don't talk** *about* **religion** *in a* **rude way**. *Ecuadorians tend to be quite religious.*

Culture

PANECILLO
(QUITO)

BASIC INFORMATION

1. **Spanish** is the **official language** of Ecuador. **Fourteen other languages** are spoken. In the Amazon: Quichua, Shuar-Achuar-Shiwiar, Wao Tededo, A'ingae, Paikoka, Zápara, and Andoa. In the highlands Quichua is present. On the coast: awapit, cha'fiki, tsa'fiki, and epera pedede.

2. Quito is the **second highest capital** city in the **world** after La Paz, Bolivia.

3. **Religion** is an important part of Ecuadorian culture. **Seventy-four percent** of the population is **Catholic**, 10% are evangelical and 8% have no religious affiliation.

4. Located on the west coast of South America. It is bordered to the north by Colombia, to the east and south by Peru and to the west by the Pacific Ocean and has maritime borders with Panama and Costa Rica.

5. Ecuador is a **democratic republic**. The **president** is elected by popular vote every **4 years** and can be reelected for a second term.

Safety *in Ecuador*

1. Always **be aware** of your **surroundings**. Don't spend too much time distracted on the street.

2. **Don't walk** around with your **phone** in your **hand**. Phone robberies with the threat of a gun are common.

3. **Don't walk** at **night** in **Quito**, **Guayaquil** or Cuenca (although this city is safer). Ask for a **cab**.

4. **Look** at **both sides** of the **street** before crossing. Cars often do not respect pedestrian crossings.

5. **Take care** of your **belongings** on **bus rides**. Do not leave your belongings on the top of the bus or on the floor. There are thieves posing as passengers. Carry your most important items on your lap.

6. **Order cabs** through **apps** such as Didi or Uber. Or ask your hotel to send you a safe cab. Cabs on the street are not always so safe.

7. **Buy** yourself a **phone chip** as soon as you arrive in the country. It is important to have internet in compromising situations, to be able to call local numbers in case of emergency, order a cab or view maps.

8. **Be careful** with your **surroundings** when withdrawing money from **ATMs**. It is safer if you do it in supermarkets or shopping malls.

9. **Avoid walking** in areas that are not very touristy, **lonely** or at night.

10. Except in Quito and Guayaquil, it is **not recommended** that you drink **tap water** in Ecuador.

11. Ecuador is located in a seismic zone. Therefore, be aware of **earthquakes** and volcano eruptions.

12. **Stay hydrated** and **wear sunscreen**. Ecuador is located in one of the closest points of the planet to the sun. Therefore, it is important to protect your skin and drink water constantly.

13. **Beware** of **rockslides** in the mountains. They are frequent during the **rainy season**.

14. In the **Amazon** there is the possibility of contracting **malaria, dengue** and **yellow** fever.

Basic words
in Spanish

Even though you won't learn Spanish in 2 days, it's always nice to arrive in a new country and use a few words in the local language. You can **learn** some **Spanish** with **Duolingo** for free.

Buenos días / Buenas tardes	**GOOD MORNING / GOOD EVENING**
Entiendo / No entiendo	**I UNDERSTAND / I DON'T UNDERSTAND**
Thank you (very much)	**MUCHAS GRACIAS**
Mi nombre es...	**MY NAME IS...**
¿Cuánto cuesta?	**HOW MUCH IS IT?**
¿Me puedes ayudar?	**CAN YOU HELP ME?**
¡Es demasiado caro!	**IT IS TOO EXPENSIVE!**
¿Dónde está? ¿ Cómo ir a…?	**WHERE IS? /HOW CAN I GET TO?**
¡Buen provecho !	**ENJOY YOUR MEAL**

Guagua pan/ Colada morada

The drink 'colada morada' is traditionally drunk on All Saints' Day. It is taken together with guagua de pan (representations of the dead wrapped in a blanket).

Typical Foods

Ceviche

Dish of raw fish or **seafood** cut in small pieces, prepared with lemon juice, chopped onion, salt, bell pepper and cilantro.

Encebollado

A typical dish from the **coastal region**. It is a **fish broth** prepared with albacore, yucca, tomato, red onion, cilantro and chili powder among other ingredients.

Hornado

A dish containing **baked pork** (cooked in firewood), accompanied by corn, avocado, lettuce and tomato. Although the latter usually vary depending on the area.

Bolón verde

A typical dish of the **coast**, ideal for **breakfast**. It is prepared with green or male plantains, stuffed with cheese, chicharrón or chorizo. It is usually accompanied by fried eggs and coffee.

Fruits

Ecuador is the **largest exporter** of **bananas** in the world. It also has other typical fruits such as **pineapple, mango, papaya** or **passion fruit**.

Acknowledgements

Agradecimientos

page

All of these people and sites also helped make
this book possible.

GRAPHIC DESIGN

Alejandra Sarmiento

—— PICTURES ——

Unsplash.com

iStock.com

— ICONS & DRAWINGS —

flaticon.com

BOOK AUTHOR

Alberto Barambio Canet

Thank you for reading my Ecuador travel guide. If you enjoyed the book, please leave a **review** on **Amazon**. Your feedback may help others discover the book - thanks for your help!

Enjoy the trip to the fullest!

Alberto

If you want to learn more about my travels, take a look at:

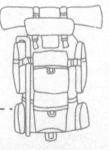

- LINKTR.EE/1HOURTRAVELGUIDES
- 1HOURTRAVELGUIDES